ESSENTIAL 101 TIPS

HIKING

ESSENTIAL 101 TIPS

HIKING

Hugh McManners

LONDON, NEW YORK, MELBOURNE,
MUNICH AND DELHI

Editor Richard Hammond
Art Editor Martin Hendry
Managing Editor Gillian Roberts
Category Publisher Mary-Clare Jerram
DTP Designer Sonia Charbonnier
Production Controller Luca Frassinetti
US Editor Jill Hamilton

First American Edition, 1998
This paperback edition published in the United States in 2004
by DK Publishing, Inc.
375 Hudson Street, New York, NY 10014
Penguin Group (US)

A catalog record is available from the Library of Congress

ISBN 0–7566–0614–4

Color reproduced in Singapore by Colourscan
Printed in China by WKT

Discover more at
www.dk.com

ESSENTIAL TIPS

101

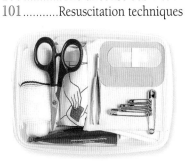

PREPARING TO WALK

1 WALKING IN THE GREAT OUTDOORS

There are few more rewarding ways of exploring the great outdoors than hiking along a wilderness trail. Enjoying the fresh air, the scenery, and the company of fellow walkers is healthy and therapeutic. There's also the excitement of a challenge: even for the most experienced walker, discovering what lies over the next hill or navigating a previously unexplored route provide a sense of adventure.

THE SPIRIT OF ADVENTURE
Walking through unknown territory is both a challenge and an adventure.

SHARED EXPERIENCE
Walking in a group allows you to share the experiences of the trail.

2 CHOOSING COMPANIONS

Although walking on your own has its own benefits of solitude and peace, it is safer to walk in a group. Walking with friends is preferable: strangers may prove unamenable or unreliable. Joining a walking association is a safe way of walking in a group, since it will usually include experienced walkers. If you join an unknown group, make an effort to talk to everyone early on.

3 ROUTE INFORMATION

A good map is indispensable. It gives you a bird's-eye view of the ground so you can plan your route and determine your position.

Before you set out, check that your map is a suitable scale (*Tip 37*), that it is up to date, and that you are familiar with the key.

1:50,000 is a useful map scale for walkers

Simple line drawing shows local trail

△ **LOCAL MAPS**
Local maps are usually lightweight leaflets that describe specific walks. They often give extra information about interesting landmarks and wildlife along each trail.

△ **OFFICIAL MAPS**
There are numerous kinds of official maps, produced to various scales and levels of detail. All official maps give information about topography and other geographical features. Information on local rights of way is usually included.

Protect map by keeping it in a waterproof case

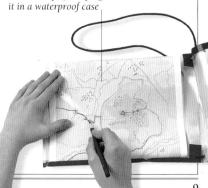

4 ASSESS YOUR HEALTH & FITNESS

Carrying a backpack on a long walk over wild terrain can be very tiring, even for the fittest walker. Make sure that the planned distance and pace of your walk is well within your capabilities as well as those of other members of your group.

DEVELOPING YOUR FITNESS
Stretching exercises help to develop suppleness and aerobic exercises, such as swimming, improve the efficiency of your heart and lungs.

Stomach toning improves body fitness

5 SAFETY FIRST

Safety must be your first concern on the walk. Before you set off, you should always let someone know where you are going, how long you intend to be away, and how many members are in your group. Take an emergency signaling device with you, so that you can let rescuers know where you are if you do find yourself in trouble.

◁ HELIOGRAPH
A heliograph is a reflective surface that you can use to flash sunlight to attract attention.

△ WHISTLE
Three blasts (long, short, long) on a whistle signal help is required.

Flashing light is a useful signal in the dark

△ STROBE LIGHT
Rescuers can see strobes 2 miles (3 kilometers) away from you.

Use eyehole to direct flash toward rescuers

SIGNALING
Carrying a signaling device could help save a friend's life.

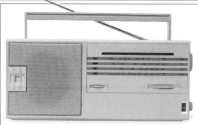
LISTEN FOR STORM REPORTS

6 CHECKING THE WEATHER FORECAST

Always find out the latest weather forecast before you go on your trip. Any of the following will give you an up-to-date forecast: newspapers, television, radio, Internet, and local or national meteorological office.

7 STAYING OVERNIGHT

If you are walking just for the day, always aim to finish the walk before sunset. If you decide to stay out in the wild overnight, you need to plan beforehand where you are going to stay. Established campsites usually have a freshwater supply and toilets. Some walkers prefer to park their car near a campsite and do a short, but very safe, night walk to the campsite where they prepare to begin walking at dawn.

SLEEPING OUT IN THE OPEN
If you sleep out in the open, choose level ground that is free of natural hazards; even dry gullies can flood if it rains.

CAMPING OUT
At a campsite, keep noise to a minimum and try to be considerate of other campers. Check whether you need to reserve ahead.

SHELTERING IN A MOUNTAIN HUT
Mountain huts provide shelter against the elements. They usually have beds, a fire-place, and sometimes emergency rations.

11

WHAT TO WEAR

8 THE LAYERING PRINCIPLE

The best fabrics insulate you from the cold, yet allow your body to shed heat and moisture. Multiple layers of thin clothing are far more effective at trapping air against your skin (to be warmed by your body) than a few thick layers. Adjust your body temperature by layering clothes.
- Wear cotton undergarments in mild weather, thermal underwear in below-freezing temperatures.
- Long pants should allow freedom of movement, and be made of a fabric that will dry quickly if it gets wet.

Hood of outer layer protects head

△ CORE LAYER
This close-fitting layer should be a material that can wick perspiration away from the skin. Use a cotton undershirt or thermal top.

△ SECOND LAYER
This layer is loose-fitting, but should be close enough to protect the neck and wrists. It could be a collared shirt or zippered polo-neck.

△ THIRD LAYER
This layer could be a woolen pullover or fleece jacket. If it's mild, this could be the outer layer, but keep a water-proof top at hand.

△ OUTER LAYER
This layer is a jacket that is either waterproof or wind-proof, or both. You must be able to vent the jacket to prevent overheating.

9 THE DOUBLE-P SYSTEM

This excellent innovation in outdoor clothing is a development of the layering system. In the double-P system, there are just two layers: a core layer that is fiber **pile**, and an outer **Pertex®** layer. Fiber pile keeps you warm, even when wet, and Pertex® offers protection since it is both windproof and showerproof, yet breathable.

10 KEEPING COOL

In hot conditions, wear lightweight, loose-fitting clothing that covers your body. Short pants and short-sleeved shirts keep you cool, but give exposed body parts no protection against harmful ultraviolet radiation.

11 KEEPING DRY

Carry waterproof clothing with you to help keep you dry in wet conditions. Make sure it covers the body from head to foot and that it is comfortable to wear. Put it on as soon as it starts to rain; take it off right after the rain stops.

Wide-brimmed hat protects head and neck from sun

Sunglasses protect eyes from UV rays

Core layer is lightweight cotton T-shirt

Second layer is lightweight shirt

Outer layer is lightweight, windproof jacket

Loose-fitting cotton pants

Lightweight boots allow feet to breathe and have heavy-duty soles for support

Hood restricts vision and hearing, so use only in heavy rain or strong winds

When resting, keep jacket zipped up. When walking, unzip it to vent clothing

In rain, zip up all pockets so they do not fill up with water trickling down from jacket

Wear waterproof overpants in driving rain

BREATHABLE GEAR
It is important that your waterproof gear not only stops water penetrating into your clothing but also allows sweat to escape from your skin.

NECK PROTECTION ▷
Pin a dishtowel to a cap to protect your neck from the sun.

Fully waterproof boots can cause feet to overheat; gaiters are a better choice

12 KEEPING WARM

In cold conditions, it is vital that you follow one of the clothing layering systems (*Tips 8 & 9*). Be prepared to vent or remove clothing if you become overheated, since trapped sweat will greatly reduce the insulating properties of your clothes.

Balaclava covers head, much of face, and neck

Polo-necked shirt should overlap balaclava at back

Thermal vest and long underwear absorb sweat

Fleece absorbs perspiration, yet still traps warm air against body

Inner gloves prevent hands from sticking to frozen objects

Hooded parka should have shell of water-resistant, breathable fabric

Ski pants are often worn over pants; they extend over waist, while allowing venting of upper body

Snow boots have plastic shell, with thermal liners as inner boots

PROTECT YOUR HEAD
In cold, wet, or windy conditions, convection from your head can cause the loss of up to half of your body heat. Wearing a hat will therefore help retain much of your body heat.

Join gloves together so they don't separate

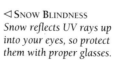

◁ SNOW BLINDNESS
Snow reflects UV rays up into your eyes, so protect them with proper glasses.

LAYERS OF GLOVES ▷
The layering system also applies to gloves. Wear heavy gloves over thinner ones.

13 CHOOSING YOUR FOOTWEAR

When choosing footwear, consider terrain, distance of walk, and the load you intend to carry.

If you are camping, take a change of footwear with you to give your feet a rest when you reach camp.

▽ **LEATHER BOOTS**
These heavy-duty boots are suitable for long-distance walking. They have strong soles and ankle supports.

▽ **CROSS TRAINERS**
Use these for short walks, as long as the terrain is not too difficult. They're also good for wearing around the camp.

▽ **SANDALS**
Though comfortable and fine for short walks in hot weather, sandals give little support or protection.

△ **FABRIC BOOTS**
These are good to wear over short distances, provided the terrain is not rough. They dry out quickly.

△ **DESERT BOOTS**
These have tough soles and lightweight suede uppers, allowing the feet to breathe while keeping out hot sand.

△ **SNOW BOOTS**
These heavily insulated boots hold the feet rigid while using crampons for grip on ice and snow.

14 WEARING IN YOUR BOOTS

Footwear must always be worn in before being used on a long walk. Before your trip, wear new footwear around the house and, if possible, go for short walks in them. If time is short, soak leather boots and wear them wet until they dry. On the trip, inspect your feet several times a day, attending to any discomfort before it becomes a serious problem (*Tip 18*).

WAX

WATERPROOFING
Leather boots should be waterproofed gradually as part of wearing them in. Use either a silicone-type spray or wax.

SILICONE-TYPE SPRAY

15 CLEANING YOUR BOOTS

If you keep your boots clean, they will last much longer and retain their waterproofing ability. It is particularly important to remove peat, since it has an acid content that can damage leather.

1 Remove the laces and inner soles, then wash off all traces of mud from the boots.

2 Allow the boots to dry. Keep them away from direct heat that could crack the leather.

3 Waterproof the dry boots, rubbing in with a finger or spraying. Store in a cool place.

16 CHOOSING SOCKS

When choosing socks, consider what your expected walking conditions will involve. Thick woolen socks insulate your feet against the ground. Thin socks soak away sweat, and may be worn over thicker socks to protect them from wear.

◁ SUMMER SOCKS
Socks for summer hiking have thick soles for insulation and padding, and thin uppers to minimize sweating. This kind of sock dries quickly after getting wet.

◁ LONG SOCKS
Knee-length woolen socks protect your legs from scratches when you walk in short pants.

◁ LOOP-STITCH SOCKS
Pull old socks over loop-stitch winter socks to protect them from wear. Loop-stitch socks can be hard on the feet, so wear softer inner socks underneath.

INNER SOCK

LOOP-STITCH SOCK

OUTER SOCK

WINTER PADDED SOCKS ▷
Thicker outer socks insulate the feet and pad them against your boots. Underneath, wear thin socks to wick moisture away.

17 GAITERS & BOOT BANDS

Waterproof footwear can make the feet overheat and sweat, causing wrinkling, blisters, and fungal infections. Gaiters are preferable because they allow the feet to breathe, yet still keep out mud, water splashes, and snow.

Closed top prevents snow getting into boot

Closed bottom keeps water out of boot

MUD GAITER

SNOW GAITER

Pull pant-ends over bands and tuck excess fabric back under them

USING BOOT BANDS △
Wet pant-ends cause discomfort as you walk. Tucking the ends into your boots is not comfortable, so use boot bands to prevent them from slipping down.

18 CARING FOR YOUR FEET

Your feet bear both your weight and that of your load. Not only must you harden your feet by wearing in your boots properly (*Tip 14*), but you must also look after them during the walk. Keep them clean, wash them at least once a day, and dust them with powder. A long walk will tire the muscles and bones of the feet, so give them a massage at the end of the day.

WASHING
Wash your feet and toenails at least once every day.

DRYING
Dry your feet vigorously with a rough towel or rag, then give them an airing.

MASSAGING
To relieve tiredness, grasp each foot with both hands and rub with the thumbs.

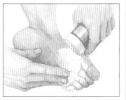

POWDERING
Rub antifungal foot powder in between your toes to prevent athlete's foot.

WHAT TO TAKE

19 CHOOSING YOUR EQUIPMENT

Buying outdoor gear for your trip can be a bewildering and costly experience, especially if you have never hiked or camped before. Start looking early and research your needs very thoroughly. In specialized outdoor shops sales assistants are usually very helpful, but be wary of being talked into unnecessary and expensive items.

PLENTY OF CHOICE
Only buy equipment that you will really need for the walk. Ask other walkers for their advice, and examine all equipment for flaws before buying it.

QUALITY GEAR
Sometimes, it is worth spending a little extra for gear that is easier to use and will last longer.

20 KINDS OF PACKS

There are many kinds of packs, ranging from small, lightweight day packs to framed, high-capacity backpacks. Choose a pack that is suitable for the sort of walking you will be doing, bearing in mind how much gear you will take with you.

Weight should be carried high on the shoulders

Adjustable straps allow the pack to be carried high on the back

A padded hip belt allows some of the weight to be transferred from shoulders to pelvis, easing pressure on the spine

ADULT'S BACKPACK ▷
Keep the backpack's center of gravity as high as possible to prevent the backpack from pulling you back. Your legs should do all the work of carrying the pack.

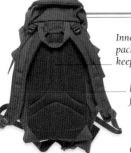

Inner frame holds
pack away from back,
keeping you cool

Padded back
for comfort

◁ **CHILD'S PACK**
Smaller packs for
children have the
same basic design
as adult day packs.
Weight belts help
keep the weight off
the shoulders.

Crocodile clips
for easy access

DAY PACKS
A light day pack should
be large enough to take
all you need for a day's
walk, including food,
water, waterproofs
and warm clothing,
maps, compass,
camera, and your
emergency equipment.

Basic straps for
adjusting tightness
on shoulders

APPROPRIATE SIZE
Choose a suitable size
pack that will hold all
you need without
having to strap any
gear to the outside.

▽ **CLIMBING PACK**
Climbing packs are no
wider than the wearer's
shoulders, although extra
capacity can be added by
attaching side pockets.

Pocket unclips
and slides off
for storage in
camp, while
pack is used
for climbing

CONVERTIBLE PACK
These backpacks can
be used to carry the
weight on the shoulders
by means of a shoulder
strap. They also double
as a luggage bag with a
carrying handle.

21 FITTING A BACKPACK

Most backpacks allow plenty of adjustment for both shape and size. Before you first use your pack, weight it with a dummy load and get to know how all the fittings work.

1 With a new or unfamiliar backpack, first loosen all the straps, noting their purpose and where the tabs are located.

Note how much slack there is for each strap

2 Fully extend the back adjustment system so that, later on, you will need only to tighten it.

3 Put on the backpack, and tighten the lower shoulder straps until the pack feels comfortable.

5 Tighten the waist strap to transfer the weight from your shoulders via your pelvis to your legs.

6 Tighten the upper shoulder straps to raise the backpack's center of gravity.

4 Adjust the back strap so that the pack is sitting as high as possible on your shoulders.

7 Tighten the shoulder straps and loosen the waist strap to relieve the pressure on your waist.

22 PACKING YOUR BACKPACK

A loaded backpack needs to be well balanced, with heavy items uppermost and the weight bearing directly downward, not pulling your shoulders back or making you hunch forward. Make sure you pack only essential items that ideally have more than one use.

A WATERPROOF PACK
Line the pack with a plastic sack to safeguard it from wet weather.

Keep first-aid kit handy at all times

Put heavy billycan set toward top of backpack

Pack tent poles and pegs together

Use soft items to pad out back of backpack

Bottom of backpack is filled out with sleeping bag

Keep wash kit in waterproof bag

Pack things inside each other to save space

Roll up clothes

PACK ORGANIZATION
Pack those items you will need for the day toward the top and outside of the pack.

23 BELT BAG

A belt bag is a very useful holder to carry around your waist. It enables easy access to personal gear, while bigger items are carried in a day pack. The bag cannot be worn with a backpack, however, since it prevents the use of the pack's waist strap.

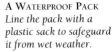

COMPASS ▽

△ SUN BLOCK   △ MONEY   △ CANDY   △ KNIFE

Water bottle fits tightly in holder

△ SUNGLASSES   ◁ WHISTLE

24 CHOOSING A SLEEPING BAG

Your sleeping bag must suit the season of your walk. A down-filled bag is lightweight and warm, but it can lose its insulation when wet; a synthetic bag is heavier, but will keep you warm even when wet.

◁ ROUNDED-FOOT BAG
The extended hood prevents heat from escaping from the head, neck, and shoulders. The zipper provides access to the bag, and the draw-string keeps out the cold.

ZIPLESS BAG ▷
With the drawstring pulled tight around the head, this style of bag minimizes heat loss. However, the lack of a zipper makes it difficult to get into and out of the bag.

25 SLEEPING ACCESSORIES

If you have space in your backpack, consider including the following accessories.

- A cotton liner, to trap a layer of warm air around you and keep your sleeping bag clean and dry.

- A sleeping mat, to support you and insulate you from the ground.
- An inflatable pillow, to provide comfort for your head.
- A foil blanket, to reduce heat loss (vital in an emergency).

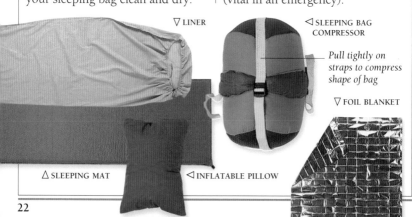

▽ LINER

◁ SLEEPING BAG COMPRESSOR

Pull tightly on straps to compress shape of bag

▽ FOIL BLANKET

△ SLEEPING MAT

◁ INFLATABLE PILLOW

26 WHICH KIND OF TENT?

Choose a tent that is well suited to your expected conditions. Ridge tents are the best-proven type, and may be used anywhere, while a dome tent (especially a geodesic dome tent) will better withstand strong winds and heavy snow. Tents with external poles are easier to pitch in high winds than those with internal poles. Two-hooped tents may prove to be unstable in extreme weather.

RIDGE TENT
This kind of tent has a built-in groundsheet, a ventilated inner tent, and a waterproof flysheet.

Short rear pole allows back of tent to present small face to wind

Tall front pole allows easy access and exit

Impermeable flysheet

Adjustable guylines support tent and poles

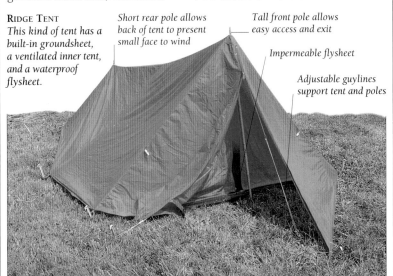

DOME TENT
This requires firm pegging in the wind, but it is less cramped than a ridge tent. Geodesic domes have interlocking poles for stability.

SINGLE-HOOPED TENT
This lightweight tent provides ample living space, and is easy to erect. Its sloping profile deflects oncoming winds.

TUNNEL TENT
This spacious tent has a frame of up to three hoops, usually with smaller hoops at each end. Many have an entrance at either end.

27 COOKING STOVES

Make sure your stove has a controllable flame that lights easily and burns fuel efficiently. Cooking areas must be well ventilated, since stoves use up oxygen and give off potentially lethal carbon monoxide. Pressurized stoves can flare up, so never lean over one, or use it for cooking inside a tent or near an unfurled flysheet.

Small pan supports

MINI STOVE ▷
This ultra-lightweight stove burns a butane/propane mixture that cannot be used below freezing. (Not suitable for large pots or pans.)

Fuel is put in stove via funnel port

MULTIFUEL ▷
A very popular stove, this model can be used to cook a meal on white gas, paraffin, or aviation fuel.

Foldaway supports

◁ GENERAL-PURPOSE
This fast-burning stove is for all-round use, and has foldaway supports for cooking with large pans.

Stove provides stable pan support

◁ NONPRESSURIZED
This very stable stove has a wind-shield, but is slow burning. It uses methylated alcohol.

28 FUELS FOR STOVES

Check that the kind of fuel you take with you is compatible with your stove. Your fuel bottles must be easily distinguishable from all your water bottles so that there is no risk of confusing them. They should be absolutely free from leaks, since leaking fuel could pollute food and rot clothes and equipment.

△ JELLY ALCOHOL

△ PARAFFIN BOTTLE   △ GASOLINE BOTTLE   △ BUTANE CARTRIDGE

29 UTENSILS FOR COOKING & EATING

Your pack weight is the main consideration when selecting utensils. The bare minimum is a spoon, mug, cooking pot, and a bowl for hot food. A kettle, plates, and even a skillet can be added, particularly with a group. Hot metal utensils can burn hands and lips, so choose plastic as a safer option for bowls and mugs.

Plate cools food for eating while rest of meal stays warm in pot

△ PLASTIC PLATE

△ PLASTIC MUG

△ PLASTIC BOWL

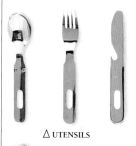

Lightweight aluminum skillet is useful for cooking in a group

Aluminum billycan set saves space, but avoid taking more pans than you need

△ UTENSILS

△ SKILLET

△ KETTLE

◁ ALUMINUM FOIL

△ BILLYCAN SET

WASHING UP
Keep all utensils scrupulously clean. Dirty dishes and scraps of food will attract flies and other unwelcome pests (Tip 79).

25

30 PORTABLE FOODS

You can carry food on your trip in a number of ways: in cans, dehydrated in containers, or in its natural state. Canned foods are ready to eat (hot or cold), but heavy to carry. Dehydrated foods are much lighter, but need time to prepare and water to rehydrate. Food in its natural state is convenient, but fruit, for example, easily bruises or squashes, and can be very messy.

DRIED FRUITS

OATS

△ BREAKFAST FOODS
Breakfast provides a vital source of energy and vitamins at the start of the day. Oats, muesli, and dried fruits are nutritious, and the fiber they contain prevents the digestive tract from clogging up.

DEHYDRATED ICE CREAM

FRUIT-FLAVORED HARD CANDIES

△ HIGH-CALORIE FOODS
Sweet foods help maintain blood sugar levels, providing energy and keeping you warm. Hard candies are good to suck on for the extra calories they yield.

FREEZE-DRIED MEAL

DRIED SOUP

△ MAIN MEALS
Dehydrated meals are ideal as a main meal, since they contain a balance of foods in one mixture. Freeze-drying dehydrates food in a way that leaves its texture intact.

INSTANT COFFEE

TEA BAGS

△ HOT DRINKS
Hot drinks have little nutritional value, but they do provide warmth and comfort. Dried milk, however, is a good source of calcium, and adding sugar boosts energy levels.

RED KIDNEY BEANS

BROWN RICE

△ RICE, BEANS, & PULSES
Rice, beans, and pulses are nutritious complements to your main meal: beans and pulses supply protein and fiber, and rice provides energy-rich carbohydrates.

APPLE   CANDY

△ **TRAIL SNACKS**
Carry snacks to nibble during the day to maintain energy and allay hunger. Save your big meal until the evening so that you can digest it thoroughly while you sleep.

PASTA MEAL   CANNED SARDINES

△ **MEAT & FISH**
Meat and fish are good sources of protein. Carry them as a meal prepared with pasta and vegetables, or canned. Always eat canned food immediately after opening.

TOMATO PASTE   STOCK CUBES

△ **MIXERS & FLAVORINGS**
Try to include some ingredients that will add spice and flavor to your meals, especially if you plan to carry all of your food in dehydrated form.

31 FOOD STORAGE

Transfer your foods from heavy glass jars to light plastic containers before you set off, to reduce your load and safeguard your stores against breakage. The plastic containers should be flexible and strong, preferably transparent, with wide necks and watertight lids.

△ **AVOIDING WASTE**
Carry your food in airtight, plastic tubs to prevent it from crumbling or spilling.

ALL-IN-ONE ▷
For accessibility, put small objects together in a single container.

Pad out spaces with tea bags

◁ **PUT A LID ON IT**
Store powdered foods in jars with screw-on lids.

32 WATER EQUIPMENT

Pure water is vital to health, so take suitably sized containers that hold plenty of water. Keep all water containers clean to prevent any contamination. It is very important that drinking water (*Tip 74*) does not contain any impurities, so make sure that you carry filtering equipment and purifying tablets with you.

◁ **PORTABLE FILTER**
This minifilter does not take up much space in your backpack and is very easy to use.

▽ **CONTAINERS**
Water containers range from rigid plastic or steel bottles to collapsible bags that can be folded up when empty. They must be easily distinguishable from fuel containers.

COLLAPSIBLE CANTEEN   BOTTLE WITH CAP   STEEL BOTTLE

◁ **LARGE WATER BAG**

TABLETS ▷
Chlorine-based tablets are a safe purifying agent.

33 USEFUL EQUIPMENT

It takes experience to learn just which items are essential for a walking trip and which are best left behind. Modifications to your gear will suggest themselves. After each trip, discard anything you did not use, and add only items that you really wished you had taken. Multi-purpose items are particularly useful because they save on packing space.

MAGNIFYING GLASS ▷

△ INSECT REPELLENT   △ WRITING EQUIPMENT   △ SUN BLOCK

△ **RADIO**

△ SPARE BATTERIES

△ **COMPACT CAMERA**
A lightweight compact camera will enable you to keep a photographic record of your trip. Secure it in an accessible part of your pack, and remember to take extra film with you.

Wood saw

Large blade

Can opener

Scissors *Nail file*

△ SWISS ARMY KNIFE
A Swiss army knife is useful because it is a small, multipurpose tool. Make sure that it has a sharp, solid blade.

△ BINOCULARS

Swivel handle ensures firm grip of hot dishes

△ SEWING KIT

△ SLEEPING MAT REPAIR KIT

△ HOT DISH HANDLE

▷ VACUUM FLASK

Handle position can be altered for steep walks

◁ ADJUSTABLE WALKING STICK

△ SCOURER

△ WASHING-UP LIQUID

△ DISH TOWEL

△ TOILET PAPER

△ ELASTIC BANDS

△ SCREWGATE CARABINER

Screw-in gate ensures that rope is attached securely (Tip 63)

◁ STRING

▷ WATERPROOF MATCHES

△ ROPE

▷ CANDLE

△ GARBAGE BAGS
Use garbage bags to keep clothes dry, as well as to store trash. They are also useful for sitting on wet ground.

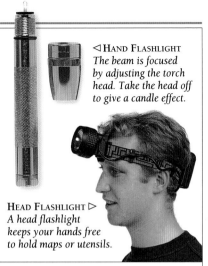

34 THE IMPORTANCE OF LIGHT

Away from the glare of city lights, nighttime in the wilderness is very dark. It is therefore important – especially if there is no moon – to carry a flashlight. Flashlights range from very small, soft-beamed kinds to heavy, wide-beamed ones. Ideally, you should carry a flash-light that is small and has a strong beam. Store it inside a plastic bag, even if it is waterproof. Remember to take suitable spare batteries.

◁ HAND FLASHLIGHT
The beam is focused by adjusting the torch head. Take the head off to give a candle effect.

HEAD FLASHLIGHT ▷
A head flashlight keeps your hands free to hold maps or utensils.

35 PERSONAL HYGIENE

Good personal hygiene is doubly important in the wild. Thorough washing helps prevent minor cuts from becoming infected, and medicated shampoo prevents infestation of your hair and scalp. Keep your washing and personal gear in a waterproof bag so you have easy access to each item, and do not lose any.

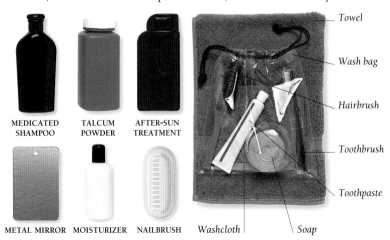

MEDICATED SHAMPOO

TALCUM POWDER

AFTER-SUN TREATMENT

METAL MIRROR   MOISTURIZER   NAILBRUSH   Washcloth

Towel

Wash bag

Hairbrush

Toothbrush

Toothpaste

Soap

36 FIRST-AID KIT

"First aid" describes the stabilization of a victim before the journey to proper medical care. Before your trip, make sure you are familiar with your first-aid kit and you know how to use the various items in an emergency. If possible, take a course in first aid; it could save a person's life.

ANTISEPTIC WIPES & CREAM

△ **ADHESIVE BANDAGES**
Adhesive bandages keep dirt from infecting cuts. Bind them over blisters with tape to keep them from being rubbed off.

Cut strips of felt to fit over any sore spots on the feet

◁ FOOT FELT

△ **FOOT CARE**
A foot felt helps to prevent a small blister from becoming a major problem. Cut foot felt to fit over the sore spot, then secure the felt with an adhesive bandage.

△ **ANTISEPTICS**
Antiseptic wipes help clean a wound. Antiseptic cream will soothe it and promote healing.

▽ **TABLETS**
Carry salt tablets for dehydration (Tips 94 & 97) and ibuprofen, acetaminophen, or aspirin for treating pain.

◁ SALT TABLETS

△ CREPE BANDAGE △ GAUZE BANDAGE △ GAUZE DRESSING △ GAUZE PADS

△ SCISSORS

△ TWEEZERS

GAUZE & BANDAGES
Gauze pads are used to absorb blood away from wounds. Bandages help keep dressings in place, bind wounds closed, and splint broken limbs.

◁ SAFETY PINS

TRIANGULAR BANDAGE ▷

SPECIAL MEDICATION
If you are on special medication, e.g., for treating asthma or diabetes, ensure that you take it with you, and include enough backup supplies.

FINDING YOUR WAY

37 UNDERSTANDING MAPS

The scale of a map can be found in the key, usually as a ratio of one unit of measurement on the map to a given number of such units on the ground. For instance, a useful scale for walkers is 1:50,000. This means that one inch on the map is equivalent to one mile on the ground, or one centimeter is equivalent to two kilometers.

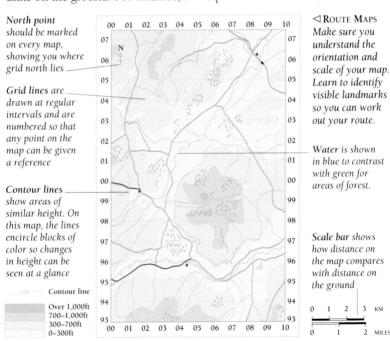

North point should be marked on every map, showing you where grid north lies

Grid lines are drawn at regular intervals and are numbered so that any point on the map can be given a reference

Contour lines show areas of similar height. On this map, the lines encircle blocks of color so changes in height can be seen at a glance

—·⁻¹⁰⁰⁻ Contour line

Over 1,000ft
700–1,000ft
300–700ft
0–300ft

◁ **ROUTE MAPS** Make sure you understand the orientation and scale of your map. Learn to identify visible landmarks so you can work out your route.

Water is shown in blue to contrast with green for areas of forest.

Scale bar shows how distance on the map compares with distance on the ground

0   1   2   3   KM

0   1   2   MILES

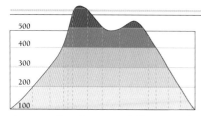

△ *Imagine lines* bisecting a hill at intervals of 300ft (100m). Draw a vertical dotted line down from the edge of each layer.

▽ *Link these lines* to form contours. Follow the lines to work out the shape of the hill.

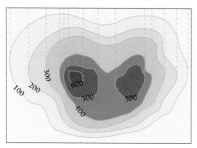

△ UNDERSTANDING CONTOURS
A contour line is an imaginary line that follows the ground surface at a specific level. Each contour line has the land height written next to it. By looking at a series of contour lines, you can see where the ground changes height. If the lines are close, the changes in land height are steep; if they are widely spaced, the change is more gradual.

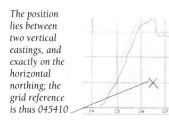

The position lies between two vertical eastings, and exactly on the horizontal northing; the grid reference is thus 045410

VALLEY
The contour lines of a valley, and the river that originally created it, appear as a complicated swirl of V-shapes.

HILL
The contour lines of a hill are recognizable as a series of ever-decreasing rings, each one a closed line.

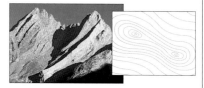

SADDLE
A saddle, which is a depression between two hills, appears as two sets of circles, joined by curving contour lines.

◁ GRID REFERENCES
Follow the vertical line left of your position to the foot of the map to read its easting. Estimate the number of tenths from the grid line to the location. Repeat with the horizontal grid line just below the location to read the northing. The saying, "first walk into the house, then climb the stairs," will remind you to state the easting first.

38 PLANNING A ROUTE

Having a purpose and time frame in mind increases the satisfaction of hiking. Your route should be well within the limitations imposed by the weather, terrain, and – if you are walking in a group (*Tip 53*) – the ability of the weakest members. When planning your route, study the map carefully, and try to talk to walkers who know the area. Keep the need for water, rest stops, and campsites firmly in mind, and try to include some enjoyable diversions.

1 △ Like any team, a walking group must have one person who assumes responsibility. Make sure that the route is flexible; as leader, you must be able to change it if anyone is struggling.

2 ▽ Identify the main objectives for your walk. Marked in orange (*below*) is a two-day walking route. Before you confirm the route, measure it roughly for distance and height, and estimate how long it might take overall (*Tip 40*), taking into account rest stops and any delays caused by poor weather. Since you will need water for your overnight stay, nominate the north end of the lake as the campsite. A revised route via this allocated site is marked in blue (*below*).

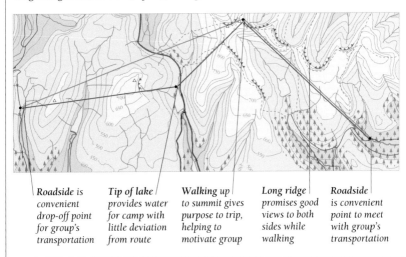

Roadside is convenient drop-off point for group's transportation

Tip of lake provides water for camp with little deviation from route

Walking up to summit gives purpose to trip, helping to motivate group

Long ridge promises good views to both sides while walking

Roadside is convenient point to meet with group's transportation

3 ▽ The direct route is now adjusted to take account of the features and obstacles along the way. On the first day, the group climbs a hill, then descends to the south of the lake to cross the dam.

The ridge is followed for a gradual ascent to the next summit, which is the day's main objective. The group then drops down to the campsite, taking a safe path along the cliffs, again using the ridgeline.

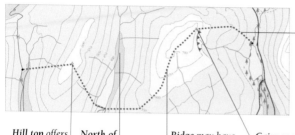

First day's walk ends by following path on ridgeline to north of cliffs, and then dropping down to campsite

Hill top offers views in all directions

North of valley may be wet

Ridge may have footpath that follows incline

Cairn may mark exact location of summit, from which you can take accurate bearings

4 ▽ The second day begins with a diversion north, to make use of a footpath to the initial summit, and then on to the second summit. The group follows the ridgeline, then walks along

the ridge down to the road. A safety route (hatched line) contours down from the ridge to the treeline. This is in case of bad weather on the high ridge, since the cliffs pose a risk in poor visibility.

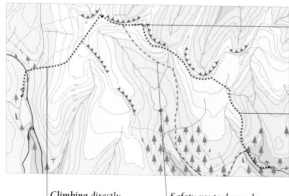

Designated route requires good visibility to avoid cliffs

Walk ends by following high ridge down to road

ESCAPE ROUTE
Always have at least one safety route planned, in case of any unexpected change in your conditions.

Climbing directly to summit may be easier in absence of nearby ridge

Safety route descends quickly and directly to road, and is planned to be suitable for carrying a victim

39 MEASURING MAP DISTANCE

Measuring map distance is vital for estimating the length of a walk, and for calculating your position. Routes rarely follow a straight course, so your technique must take bends into account.

1 Starting at a corner of a sheet of paper, align the edge with the route. Mark the first turn of the route with a sharp pencil.

2 Rotate the paper around the pencil until it aligns with the route again. Mark the next turn in the route.

3 When you reach the corner of the paper, rotate it, and then continue marking along the edge of the sheet.

4 When the route has been marked, use the key at the foot of the map to mark each mile (or kilometer) on the sheet.

NOTING LANDMARKS
As you mark each turn, note any landmarks on the way, using symbols for any features that you come across.

5 Work out the total of miles (or kilometers). Marking steep gradients will help when you come to estimate journey time.

40 ESTIMATING JOURNEY TIME

Naismith's Rule takes into account not only distance but also topography. It suggests that you should allow 60 minutes for every 3 miles (5km) traveled, adding 30 minutes to that total for every 1,000ft (300m) climbed. For descent of moderate slopes, subtract 10 minutes for every 1,000ft (300m) of height lost, but for very steep slopes add 10 minutes for every 1,000ft (300m) of height lost.

41 HOW A COMPASS WORKS

There are many different kinds of compass. All work on the same principle of the compass needle being attracted to magnetic north and magnetic south, the poles of the Earth's magnetic field.

PROTRACTOR COMPASS ▷
This kind of compass is light, very reliable, and sufficiently accurate for basic orienteering and navigation.

Direction arrow points the way when compass has been set in relation to magnetic north

Bearings are read at the point where tail of direction arrow cuts dial

Parallel lines on compass housing are aligned with the north – south grid lines on map to orientate compass

PRISMATIC COMPASS ▽
A prismatic compass is more accurate than a protractor compass. It has a luminous dial and lockable bearing scale, useful for night navigation.

Luminous strip attached to hinged lid

Graduated, movable outer ring

HOW TO USE A PRISMATIC COMPASS

1 △ Look though the eyepiece and align the hairline in the lid with the object you have chosen. Look slightly downward, and read the magnetic bearing on the disk against the hairline.

2 △ Add or subtract the local magnetic variation from your reading in order to get the grid bearing. Plot the bearing on your map, aligning 0° on the protractor to north.

3 ▽ To set a map bearing, add or subtract the magnetic variation, then set the bearing on the compass. Align the north pointers to see your direction.

Vertical hairline should bisect chosen object when sighting

42 SETTING YOUR COMPASS

To orient yourself on the ground, you must first find north (and the top of your map), and then either turn around so that you and the map are facing north, or rotate the map to point in your direction of travel. You may then set your compass on the map.

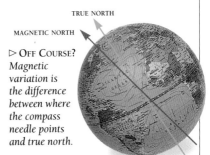

TRUE NORTH

MAGNETIC NORTH

▷ **OFF COURSE?**
Magnetic variation is the difference between where the compass needle points and true north.

1 To find the bearing from A (your position) to B (your destination), point the direction arrow from A to B. Measure the line A–B on the compass edge, and compare it with the map scale.

2 Turn the central dial until the north–south lines align with the map's grid lines. The north (red) arrow now points to grid north. This sets the bearing (the angle between A–B and magnetic north).

3 Turn the map until the north arrow aligns with magnetic north, as indicated by the needle. The direction-of-travel arrow on the compass will now point to the bearing that you have set.

4 You can now hold the compass and follow the direction-of-travel arrow. Keep the compass level, and ensure that the north (red) arrow on the dial and north on the magnetic disk are aligned.

43 LOCATING YOUR POSITION

You can locate your approximate position by choosing two or more landmarks, identifying them on the map, and orienting the map to them. Using your compass, you can take back bearings from the landmarks to get a more accurate fix on your position on the map.

1 Survey the terrain and pick out two landmarks likely to be featured on your map. These landmarks (two houses are selected here) should lie at least 20° apart from your vantage point.

2 Take a bearing to the first house. Add or subtract the magnetic variation if it is great in your area; otherwise you can usually ignore it. Identify the feature on your map.

3 With a pencil, draw a back bearing from the landmark on your map. This is done by adding or subtracting 180° from your original bearing, or by reading 180° opposite your original bearing on the dial of your compass.

4 Take a bearing to the second house. In jungle, moorland, desert, or snow, hilltops may be the only features, so use map contours to determine the location of each one.

5 Mark the second back bearing on the map, as in Step 3. Your position is where the two back bearings intersect.

44 CHECKING DIRECTION WITHOUT A COMPASS

Knowing the direction in which you are headed is the most important part of navigation. If you lose your compass, or if it breaks, do not panic – it is still possible to keep track of your direction. Follow a course using the sun during the day, and the stars at night.

45 USING THE SUN TO DETERMINE DIRECTION

The sun always rises in the east and sets in the west, so it can be used to find these two points. Use a watch in conjunction with the sun to get an indication of north or south (depending on which hemisphere you are in). If it is cloudy, align with the brightest area of the sky.

NORTHERN HEMISPHERE
Point the hour hand to where the sun is coming from. Imagine a line half-way between the hour hand and 12 o'clock. South is at the head of that line.

SOUTHERN HEMISPHERE
Point the 12 o'clock mark to where the sun is coming from. North lies halfway between the 12 o'clock mark and wherever the hour hand is on the watch.

46 NAVIGATING BY THE STARS

Stars do not move relative to each other, so they can be relied upon for use in navigation. Only one star appears not to move – the North (or Pole) Star, which is used in the Northern Hemisphere to find north. In the Southern Hemisphere, the Southern Cross is used to locate south.

NORTHERN HEMISPHERE
Extend a line from the two stars at the front of the Big Dipper (Plough) to about four times the distance between those stars to the Pole Star. This star lies over north on the horizon.

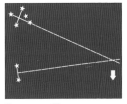

SOUTHERN HEMISPHERE
Extend a line from the crosspiece of the Southern Cross to four-and-a-half times its length. South is on the horizon below this point. The two stars shown above also help find south.

Visual display states the coordinates of your position, usually accurate to 330ft (100m)

SELECTIVE AVAILABILITY (S/A)
When US armed forces turn off S/A, a GPS is accurate to 50ft (15m) or less.

47 GLOBAL POSITIONING SYSTEM (GPS)

This system uses a collection of 24 satellites, whose radio signals may be received at any location. By tuning in to this worldwide network, you can determine your position (longitude, latitude, and altitude) and obtain a clear record of your progress. The GPS is accurate to 330ft (100m), or better, 95% of the time, and to 1,000ft (300m) the remaining 5%.

48 USING BINOCULARS

Binoculars can save much legwork, and are extremely useful for looking at wildlife and other aspects of the environment. Adjust their width and focus until you can see one sharp image, then look through them into the terrain or at the object you wish to observe. Do not look at the sun with binoculars: a magnified sun can cause blindness.

Adjust focus to get a sharp image

49 KEEPING A RECORD

Taking notes or sketching anything of particular interest on your walk can serve as a useful reminder of the trail. You may wish to keep a diary, and build a lasting chronicle of any experience that shaped your thoughts at the time. Rereading these notes at a later stage can bring immense pleasure.

△ WRITING CASE   ▷ WATERPROOF PEN

MOVING ON THE TRAIL

FOLLOWING TRAILS
Marked paths often lead you along interesting trails and to spectacular views.

50 USING MARKED PATHS

Getting lost on paths is surprisingly easy. Always use your compass to set the bearing of where you intend to go, and check it regularly. Marked paths often split into smaller tracks that tend – unfortunately – to meander, leading you somewhere completely different from your intended route.

51 RIGHTS OF WAY

Always walk around fields if there is no footpath through them; there may be crops growing, which will be someone's livelihood. Even if fields look free of crops (for example, in spring), crops may be growing underground. Do not force your way through fences or hedges; if you damage them, animals could escape.

RESPECT PATH BOUNDARIES
Do not wander off paths that border nature reserves and other areas of conservation.

GARBAGE BUILDS UP QUICKLY

52 PROTECT THE WILD

Take all of your garbage home with you. The wilderness is a fragile place that is there to be enjoyed, but it must be treated well. Remember the saying, "take only memories, leave only footsteps."

RUCKSACK SEAT
Ask someone behind you to check regularly that your baby is comfortable.

FAMILY WALKING
Remember to consider children's limitations and requirements.

53 SETTING THE PACE

When walking in a group, the walking pace should be that of the slowest members, so that they do not feel left behind, or a hindrance to others. Walk together at a steady pace, keeping the group as a unit. Even the more experienced walkers can struggle, so keep an eye on all members of the group, and propose extra rest stops if necessary.

54 REST STOPS

Designate times in the day when you stop, rest, and look around. Ideally, aim to stop every 50 minutes for about 10 minutes. Rest stops are good for morale and for checking on your position, so try to plan your stops for places that have a good view.

FLUID INTAKE
Rest stops are a good opportunity to replenish lost fluids.

GROUP REST
Time your stop from when the last one in the group sits down.

55 LUNCH & SNACKS

It is important to keep up your blood sugar level during the day. Eating little and often maintains your energy without having to stop and prepare a meal. Hot soup with crackers makes a good lunch in cold weather.

HOT DRINK OR SOUP   COOKIES   TRAIL MIX   FRESH FRUIT

56 WEATHER WATCHING

The weather is influenced by terrain, season, altitude, and latitude as well as by climate. Weather forecasting is now done using powerful computer analysis, but there are many natural clues that will help you to interpret the weather. Looking to windward, clouds can help you predict weather changes coming your way.

KINDS OF CLOUDS
Clouds are classified by height and appearance. There are three kinds: low, medium, and high.

Cirrostratus: *High, dark streaks of ice clouds that may warn of rain or snow within 15 hours*

Cumulonimbus: *The dark, flat-topped, anvil-shaped head is associated with heavy rain*

Stratocumulus: *Irregular shapes of dense gray or white cloud rarely produce more than light drizzle*

Cumulus: *Drifting puffs of white cumulus clouds against a blue sky forecast fair weather*

Stratus: *Low, shallow gray clouds produce long periods of drizzle. Cold winds can increase the precipitation*

Altostratus: *Thick gray clouds that may give rise to the first drops of rain*

Cirrus: *High, wispy clouds that indicate fair weather. In winter, cirrus with steady wind may herald snow*

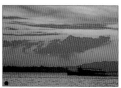

◁ **RED OR ORANGE SKY**
A red or orange sky in the evening indicates the approach of fair, sunny weather. However, a red or orange sunrise suggests rain or snow within a day.

RAINBOW
A rainbow early in the morning signals showers. A rainbow late in the day heralds fine weather.

57 WALKING TECHNIQUES

Just as boots require careful "walking in" in order to avoid discomfort and injury, walking with a backpack takes practice. You may find that you like to walk with a walking stick, which can give useful support when the terrain is difficult. When walking in a group, the golden rule is that the group must stick together. The leader may wish to appoint a second-in-command who should be a strong walker, and who brings up the rear of the group to ensure that slower walkers are not left behind.

Shape surface of stick to get a smooth finish

TAILOR-MADE WALKING STICK
Most people like a stick that extends to just above waist height, but you may prefer a longer stick.

WALKING UPHILL
Lean forward and take short steps, placing your feet flat on the ground before pushing upward. Try to avoid walking on your toes.

WALKING DOWNHILL
Take short steps and move steadily, leaning backward to take the strain off your knees. Using your stick will also relieve the strain on your knees.

STEEP SLOPES
If a slope is very steep or has a soft surface, climb it with your feet placed sideways, using your stick downhill of your body as an extra support.

45

58 WATERLOGGED GROUND

Bogs and marshes can occur anywhere, even on slopes and hilltops. In moorland, keep a lookout for sudden patches of bog. Make each footstep carefully, and try to keep to patches of firm tussock grass. Use a stick to test the ground, and be prepared to "skip" across doubtful patches.

CROSSING A BOG

59 DIFFICULT TERRAIN

Although you should try to avoid dangerous terrain, often there is simply no alternative route. Movement is considerably slowed, but safety must be your priority. Use proper techniques, take your time, and never attempt awkward terrain without good cause.

◁ SCREE
Climb sideways on scree slopes, using a stick or ski pole for extra support. Descending down scree slopes can be exciting; take hopping strides, and do your best not to lose your step.

◁ SNOW
Walking on snow is particularly treacherous, since it can be slippery underfoot. Wear snow boots (Tip 13) and crampons for extra grip, and snow gaiters to keep the snow out.

▷ SAND
Walking over sand is especially tiring, since the surface sinks with the weight of your pack and body. With each step, place your feet flat, and put weight down gradually and deliberately.

▷ BOULDER FIELDS
A slip in a boulder run while carrying a heavy backpack can break a leg, or worse. If you cannot make a detour around the boulders, move slowly, testing each foothold before you go forward.

60 NAVIGATION TECHNIQUES

Navigation has two elements: taking bearings and estimating distances. You can confirm where you are by using a compass, but factors such as rough terrain can make it difficult to stay on course.

◁ **AIMING OFF**
Following a compass bearing is accurate only to about 10° or 20°, less in rough country. If you try to walk to a fork in a river, you may not know when you reach the river whether to continue to left or right to reach the fork. By aiming off to one side, you will have no doubt where the fork is when you reach the river.

Aim to one side of your bearing

Walk along fixed height

▷ **CONTOURING**
When following a bearing, you can waste a lot of energy in repeatedly climbing up hills, only to climb down the other sides. Contouring uses the compass as a general direction reference point while you follow a contour on the map. This enables you to stay at a fixed height as you negotiate the hills between you and your objective.

"Jump off" from handrail to your destination

◁ **FOLLOWING A HANDRAIL**
If your destination lies behind a large feature, it can be impossible to take a direct bearing on it. In such cases, aim for a feature that will lead you (as a handrail would) to your destination. Walk to the feature and follow it around until you near your destination, then "jump off" the feature, on a bearing to your destination.

61 HOW TO CROSS WATER SAFELY

Before getting wet, explore up- and downstream to see if there is any kind of bridge. Failing that, look for a section of water where the riverbed is firm, and decide where it will be safest to cross. Check that the far bank is not too steep. Use footwear that has a good grip, and be wary of sudden changes in water depth.

USING A MAKESHIFT BRIDGE
If you can find a suitably sized log, lay it across the river and slowly walk across it.

Assess depth of river

Undercut bank makes climbing out of water very difficult

WIDE RIVER
Study the water before you enter it. Even if water appears to be calm and slow moving, shallow and safe, assume there are hidden dangers. Always cross slowly.

Waves that stand still are caused by strong underwater currents

FAST-FLOWING STREAM
A fast-flowing stream is dangerous to cross. If you have to cross this water, do so either in a three-person huddle or using safety ropes (Tip 63).

62 WADING ALONE

When crossing water alone, probe the bed for rocks or holes with a pole, then use it in the water as a third supporting "leg." Place the pole upstream of you and lean on it as you lift your leading foot, sliding this foot sideways across the current and replacing it firmly.

Loosen straps so pack can be discarded if you fall

Use a stout, strong pole for support

63 CROSSING WATER IN A GROUP

Crossing in a group can be safer than crossing alone because you have the support of others.

The strongest person should be upstream, taking the first steps. Link together in a huddle or in a line.

DIRECTION OF FLOW

DIRECTION OF JOURNEY

◁ IN A LINE
The weakest person should be in the middle, linked to the others for support. Cross slowly, putting each foot down deliberately.

DIRECTION OF FLOW

DIRECTION OF JOURNEY

▷ THREE-PERSON HUDDLE
Form a tripod shape, and lean in toward each other, bending forward slightly at the waist. This is a stable formation, and very effective in fast, shallow water.

△ CROSSING OVER ROCKS
Sometimes it is possible to cross over a river using rocks as stepping stones. Take off your backpack for greater balance, and use your walking stick for support.

△ CROSSING WITH ROPES
For extra support when crossing a dangerous river, clip yourself to a safety rope held by others. Wade across with a pole for further support.

△ USING A CARABINER
Clip yourself on to the safety rope with a carabiner for extra personal security.

Secure yourself by tying the rope around your waist using a figure-eight knot (Tip 64)

64 THREE USEFUL KNOTS

- Bowline: For the loop of a lifeline; it will not work itself loose.
- Figure-of-eight: For a loop that will not slip, yet is easy to untie.
- Reef: For joining lines together; it can be easily undone when wet.

BOWLINE

Take end around main rope, then bring back through small loop

1 △ Make a small overhand loop, and bring the end up through it from behind.

2 △ Take a firm hold of the two ends of the rope, then pull on both to tighten the knot.

3 △ Take end over right-hand side of loop and behind, then down into new small loop from top. Tighten against bowline.

SINGLE FIGURE-OF-EIGHT KNOT

Make knot at least 7ft (2m) from rope-end

1 △ Make an upward turn, cross behind rope, make another upward turn, then feed rope-end through the loop from the back.

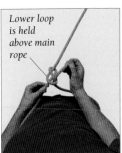

Lower loop is held above main rope

2 △ Take the short rope-end and pass it around your back. Feed from back to front, through the lower loop.

Feed end of rope through upper loop

3 △ Take the end of the rope to the left of the knot, under the main rope, then pass it from front to back, through the upper loop of the figure-of-eight.

Allow sufficient space between knot and waist

4 △ Take the rope-end to the left, curl it around the bottom of the knot, and feed it up through the upper loop of the figure-of-eight. Tighten the knot.

SQUARE KNOT

Right over left

1 △ To begin the square knot, first cross the right strand over and under the left one.

Left over right

2 △ Take the left end over and under the right strand, keeping firm hold of both ends.

3 △ Pull on both ends to tighten the knot. It can be made in reverse (left over right, right over left).

65 BEING "LOST"

Being "lost" can mean having wandered a few yards off course in thick woodland, or being several miles out of your way. Or you may believe that you had a good idea where you are, only to be confused by inaccuracies in your map. Always stop and take stock of your position before you continue to walk on.

CONSULT YOUR MAP
Use your map to establish boundaries in the surrounding area that will be recognizable if you cross them.

66 THE SPIRAL SEARCH

A spiral search is used to pinpoint a feature after arriving at an approximate position. Setting the compass to one of the four compass points, walk no further than the limit of visibility, counting your paces. If the feature is not found, turn 90° to the right and walk on for up to twice the distance. Continue, adding the distance of the first leg each time you turn. In time, the widening spiral will take you to your objective.

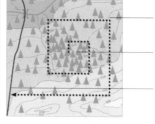

Spiral search conducted to locate pathway

Thick forest obstructs visibility

Pathway (identified on map) out of area

CAMPING OVERNIGHT

67 CHOOSING A CAMPSITE

It's a good idea to decide the general area where you intend to camp when you plan your route (*Tip 38*). Schedule your day so that you have plenty of time to choose the correct position for your camp; time spent in reconnaissance is never wasted. Many factors affect where you choose to camp, but safety should always come first.

Campsite should be close to water supply, but away from animal drinking place

If you intend to build a fire, make sure there is a source of wood nearby

Trees provide shelter from prevailing winds

Pitch tent on cleared, level ground

BUILDING A FIRE
Make a fire away from the tent, but close enough to smoke out insects.

WASHING DIRTY DISHES
Wash pots downstream from collecting water.

AN IDEAL CAMPSITE
The ideal site is close to a plentiful water supply, sheltered from prevailing winds, and on level, well-drained ground.

68 SETTING UP CAMP

Before you take your tent on a trip, practice setting it up, so that you will be able to erect it quickly if the conditions are poor; also check that it is serviceable. Once you are at the campsite, always put the tent up first, then make preparations for your stay.

Wrap drinks in cloth in water bucket to keep them cool

DRYING BOOTS ▷
Leave your boots to dry upside down, so that creatures do not crawl inside them.

△ **ERECTING YOUR TENT**
Always peg down the main part of the tent before fine-tuning the guylines.

▷ **TIGHTENING GUYLINES**
Tighten and balance both sides of the tent equally.

PLAN YOUR SCHEDULE
Make sure that you have plenty of time to put up the tent and build a fire. The tent should be up, and cooking under way, by dusk.

69 INSIDE YOUR TENT

Organize your tent so you can reach as much as possible while inside your sleeping bag. Unpack items only as you use them, repacking when finished. There should always be a layer of air between the inner tent and outer flysheet; do not allow the two to touch, or condensation may form on the inner tent, resulting in pools of water collecting in the tent.

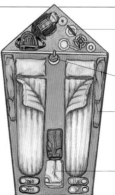

Cooking utensils laid out (packed away at night)

Light illuminates inside of tent

Waterproofs on side: condensation affects them less than other clothes

Clothing in center, away from any side condensation

70 INGREDIENTS FOR A FIRE

You will need three types of materials: tinder, kindling, and main fuel. Before building your fire, gather together far more of each type than you think you might need. Everything must be dry, so in wet weather look for sheltered materials. The best source of dry fuel is standing deadwood. If you have to use fallen wood, avoid material in contact with the ground, and take branches from on top.

BARK

FUNGUS

MOSS

DEAD LEAVES

DRY GRASS

TINDER
Tinder (bark, fungus, moss, dead leaves, or dry grass) is indispensable unless you are able to substitute a manufactured fire-lighter, such as a paraffin block (Tip 72).

◁ **KINDLING**
Kindling consists of dry leaves and small sticks. It is added to the fire once the tinder has caught and is burning.

△ **SMALL FUEL**
When the kindling is burning, add sticks that are about the width of a finger thick.

◁ **MAIN FUEL**
Large sticks act as the main fuel. They should be thicker than your finger and broken into lengths.

▷ **LARGE FUEL**
Thick logs will keep a fire going overnight. Ensure that they are fully burned when you put the fire out.

WOODS TO AVOID
Some resinous woods, such as blackthorn and pine, spit quite fiercely in a fire, and should be avoided. Other woods, such as alder, willow, and poplar, merely smolder, rather than burning well.

71 BUILDING & LIGHTING A FIRE

The secret of making a good fire is to build it up gradually, beginning with small pieces of wood, then progressing to larger branches and logs as the fire gets going.

TRENCH FIRE
The bulk of the fire is below ground level. This prevents it from flaring too fiercely but it allows a suitable supply of air.

1 △ Gather all the ingredients for the fire in one place, then remove a square of turf and put it to one side. Kneeling down next to the square, lay a platform of green sticks in the hole.

2 △ Build up a tepee by balancing upright sticks against each other, their top ends meeting in a point. Leave enough space inside for the tinder, and a suitable gap for introducing a match.

3 △ Put the tinder on the floor of the tepee and light it with a match. As the tinder catches fire, add more tinder, followed by leaves and twigs. As the heat builds up, the tepee will eventually collapse, creating a bed of hot embers.

72 WET-WEATHER FIRELIGHTERS

In dry weather, your tinder will light with just a match. It is still worth carrying another form of firelighter, however, to use if the weather suddenly becomes wet.

PARAFFIN BLOCKS

WATERPROOF MATCHES

73 LIGHTING A PRESSURE STOVE

The fuel in a pressurized stove vaporizes on release, and can be lit as soon as there is an open flow of fuel from the tank to the burner. Even though many kinds of liquid fuel can be used in these stoves, always use filtered, unleaded fuel. Before filling a stove with fuel, make sure the flame is fully extinguished.

Fuel lever controls flow of fuel from tank to burner

Stove is filled with fuel via funnel in fuel port

USE WITH CAUTION
Pressurized stoves can flare up, so never lean over one, or use inside a tent.

Lever adjusts flame height

Relock valve after pumping

1 △ Undo the pressure-lock valve, then prime the stove with 20 strokes of the pressure pump. Relock the valve.

Smear solid fuel all around burner

2 △ Stove should light immediately. If the stove is too cold, preheat it with solid fuel to enable fuel to vaporize.

Light with match

3 △ Light the solid fuel. Once the metal has warmed, open the fuel lever, and the burning solid will ignite the fuel.

Keep a firm grip on stove when adjusting flame height

4 △ Use the flame lever to select the kind of flame you want. If the flame is uncertain, pump the stove a few times.

74 PURIFYING DRINKING WATER

In the wild, water is seldom pure and should always be purified before being drunk. Even if the water looks clear, it may contain microorganisms and intestinal parasites that could make you extremely ill almost immediately.

• Always filter water to remove particles of silt and other contaminants.

• Always sterilize water to remove disease-causing waterborne microorganisms.

COLLECTING WATER
Choose your drinking water from a site that is upstream from your camp and from where any animals drink.

FILTERING WATER
Put the hose in the impure water; pump the handle. As the filtered water comes out of the spout, collect it in a clean bottle.

STERILIZING WATER
Add tablets, following packet instructions, then leave for one hour. If in doubt, boil water for at least five minutes.

WATERBORNE DISEASES

Disease	Cause	Symptoms
Leptospirosis	Animal urine or body parts infected with a bacterium.	Influenza-like (fever, chills, headache, muscle pain).
Schistosomiasis	Freshwater parasitic worm, or parasites in freshwater snails.	Itching, asthma, urinary tract irritation, liver enlargement.
Amebic dysentery	Drinking water contaminated with infected sewage.	Diarrhea with blood and/or pus, and infection of colon.
Hookworms	Parasitic larvae entering body via drinking water or the skin.	Anemia and lethargy. If in blood, may cause pneumonia.
Giardiasis	Parasitic *Giardia* in water with infected urine or feces.	Diarrhea, abdominal cramps, and nausea.

75 MAKING DINNER

Eat a hot, nutritious, and substantial meal in the evening so that you can digest it while you are sleeping. Try to make the meal as interesting and varied as possible by mixing different ingredients, and including a dessert. If you are cooking with dehydrated food, make sure that it is fully rehydrated before you eat it.

Enjoy a mug of soup as an appetizer

▷ **DRIED MEALS**
Dehydrated food requires plenty of water to rehydrate it. Never eat it dry or even partially rehydrated – it will absorb water from your body, and may cause intestinal blockages.

Sealed foil bag keeps dehydrated food fresh

△ **ALL-IN-ONE STEW**
Make all-in-one stews by combining whatever food items you have. Aim to have everything within the mixture cooked at the same time. Add cheese or a dried meal to produce a satisfying consistency.

Drink the juice of the fruit before eating it

FLAVORINGS
Pepper, spices, and herbs transform stews. Combine them with curry spices, fresh chilies, ginger, and garlic to make a delicious curry.

Fruit, such as peaches, is a refreshing dessert

◁ **DESSERT**
Many walkers use the evening meal as a chance to relax. Leave an hour between the main course and dessert so you can really enjoy the meal.

76 A BEDTIME DRINK

Drink plenty of liquids at bedtime to prevent dehydration in the night. It is better to be woken in the early morning by a full bladder than by thirst and indigestion caused by freeze-dried foods. In the cold, a sweet hot drink keeps you warm while you sleep.

HOT MILKY DRINK

77 PREPARING BREAKFAST

In the morning, combine high-energy foods with a hot drink to set you up for the day's walk. After making the drink, put any remaining hot water in your vacuum flask so that you can have another hot drink after breakfast.

HOT BLACK TEA

MAKING A HOT DRINK
When heating water on a stove, conserve fuel by placing a lid on the pan.

CEREAL

SAFEGUARDING FOOD
You can make food inaccessible to pests by hanging it up in a tree. Cover the food with a fine mesh so air can get to it but pests cannot.

DANGER
Fire is a great hazard. Keep a container of sand or soil at hand to put it out.

Hang food up in the shade to keep it cool

78 SAFE CAMPING

Good planning prevents most common campsite accidents. Many occur at night, so prepare for darkness in advance.

- When you set up the camp, visualize how it will be at night.
- Remove any clutter that you might stumble over in the dark.
- Seal your food and washing gear so that you do not attract pests to the campsite overnight (*Tip 79*).
- Make sure all cooking areas are well ventilated: cooking stoves give off carbon monoxide.
- Never lean over a pressurized stove, or use it inside a tent.

79 CAMPSITE PESTS

Even if you are staying at a campsite for just one night, you could be invaded by anything from swarms of ants or midges to hungry bears and skunks. Many of these pests are attracted by the smell of food or washing gear, so hang up these items to prevent them from acting as bait (*Tip 78*). Also, never encourage animals to return to you by feeding them, even if they seem harmless and friendly.

Tip of tail is sharp for piercing skin

Long mouthpart for sucking up blood

△ SCORPIONS
Shake your sleeping bag, boots, and clothes to eject any scorpions or spiders that may be lurking there.

△ SKUNKS
Skunk spray is vile. If a skunk comes to your camp in search of food, back off and keep clear.

△ MOSQUITOES
Mosquitoes deliver an itchy bite, so use an insect repellent, and burn a coil at night to clear your tent.

Ant jaws can give a painful nip

△ ANTS
Before you pitch camp, look for ant nests or ant trails that connect with the water.

△ BLACKFLIES
Bloodsucking blackflies have powerful jaws that can bite through clothing to get to your skin.

▽ RATS
Rats and other similar rodents are notorious scavengers for food.

INSECT PROTECTION
Use a fine-mesh mosquito net to prevent insects from biting you at night. Before you set off on your trip, treat the net with an effective insect repellent.

△ BEARS
Never feed or go near any bears, even if they appear harmless. They can be very dangerous, especially if they have cubs with them.

80 CLEARING THE CAMPSITE

Leave the campsite exactly as you found it. Take all of your trash away with you, especially any cans that will not decompose. Burn them in the fire to remove any food that could putrefy, then flatten them ready to carry away. Do not leave any scraps of food around that might attract pests to the site, and leave the site unspoiled for others to use.

FLATTENED CAN WITH ENDS INSIDE

81 CLEANING UP THE FIRE

You must make sure the fire is fully out when you finally strike camp. Even if you have filled in the fire pit, it may contain embers that are still smoldering. These have the potential to cause a forest fire.

1 When the fire has burned down, scrape the ash into the center. When the ash is cold, spread it into the ground.

2 Ensure there are no ashes on the surface to kill the grass, then fill in the fire pit with soil. Replace the original turf.

3 Fill in the edges with soil and grass, then scatter leaves and grass over the site so it looks like the surrounding area.

82 DISMANTLING THE TENT

Give yourself a deadline for leaving the campsite, and get into the habit of dismantling the tent quickly, just before you move out. In cold or wet weather, the tent must be dismantled as quickly as possible to prevent people from getting cold or wet while they stand around.

Insert tent poles into a separate bag first

Wrap up flysheet into tight rolls

PACKING THE TENT AWAY
Check that the tent's guylines are not tangled, and all the pegs have been removed from the site.

PERSONAL SAFETY

83 TAKING CARE ON THE TRAIL

The main thing to remember when you go hiking is to enjoy it. Marvel at the diversity of the wildlife, revel in the scenery – and take pleasure simply in being outdoors. It is vital to bear in mind, however, that accidents can and do occur, and you should therefore always act responsibly on the trail.

WALKING SAFELY ALONG A STEEP DROP

84 DANGEROUS CREATURES

Wild places are home to many dangerous creatures, so find out about any potentially harmful animals that you might come across on your walk. Wild animals may look like their friendly domestic relatives, but they can react violently if threatened, so keep away.

△ DINGO (WILD DOG)

◁ WASP

▷ RATTLESNAKE

Tail vibrates when snake is threatened

△ POISONOUS SPIDER

Back arches in self-defense

▽ ALLIGATOR

◁ WILD CAT

AVOID DANGER
It is better to avoid danger than to deal with it. Always respect wild animals.

85 ANIMAL BITES

An animal bite carries the risk of bacterial infection, so make sure that your tetanus vaccination is up to date, if necessary. Animals infected with the rabies virus can still appear quite normal, so treatment should always be sought after any animal bite.

With victim lying down, keep wound raised above level of heart

◁ STOP INFECTION
Pour cold water over the wound for at least 5 minutes to prevent bacterial infection.

◁ STOP BLEEDING
Apply pressure with a gauze pad to stop any further bleeding. Bandage the pad in place.

BEE STINGS
A bee often leaves its sting sac in the wound. This must be scraped out with tweezers or a knife blade.

86 INSECT STINGS

The sting from a bee, wasp, or hornet causes pain at first, followed by mild swelling and soreness. Wash with soap and water, then apply antiseptic cream.

87 DANGERS OF PLANTS & FUNGI

Eat plants and fungi in the wild only if you are certain of their identity and local rules permit. Eating unidentified plants and fungi carries considerable risk of poisoning. Examine each potential food carefully, taking note of its habitat and season of growth.

WOOD MUSHROOM

YELLOW-STAINING MUSHROOM

FOOD OR POISON?
Even experienced fungi gatherers make errors. These fungi may look similar, but the wood mushroom is edible and the yellow-staining kind is poisonous.

88 BLISTERS

Leave blisters intact: bursting them increases the risk of infecting underlying tissue. Gently clean the blisters, then pad them to prevent boots pressing on them. If you have to burst a blister, use a sterile needle to prick at its edge and let out the fluid.

89 REMOVING FOREIGN BODIES

When removing a splinter from the skin or an object from the eye, be careful not to push the foreign body further in. If you have an object in your eye, do not rub the eye, but gently separate the eyelids and examine where the object is lodged.

▷ SPLINTERS
With clean tweezers, draw the splinter out of the skin. Encourage some bleeding to flush out any dirt, wash the area, then dress the wound.

△ OBJECT IN THE EYE
Wash the eye out with clean water. If this does not work, try removing the object with a moist swab, or the dampened corner of a tissue.

90 SPRAINS & BREAKS

A sprain is a soft-tissue injury that is readily treated. Follow the "RICE" procedure for the injured part – Rest, apply Ice, Compression, Elevation. A break is more serious and should be seen by a specialist. In the mean time, immobilize the broken limb.

SPRAINED ANKLE
After the ice or cold compress, apply a padded bandage to compress the swelling. Elevate the injured limb on a firm support. Check the circulation every 10 minutes.

BROKEN LEG
Immobilize the broken leg by binding it to the good leg. Tie the knots on the good leg. Wrap a bandage around the feet and ankles to support them.

91 EXTERNAL BLEEDING

You can usually control external bleeding by direct or indirect pressure and elevation of the injured part. For severe bleeding, perform the ABC of resuscitation (*Tip 100*) and treat for shock.

SERIOUS EXTERNAL BLEEDING

Apply pressure to wound to encourage blood clotting

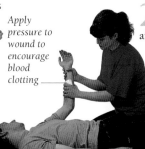

1 △ After exposing the damaged area, press the edges of the wound together and apply direct pressure.

2 ◁ Lay the victim down, and raise the affected limb above the victim's heart. Dress the wound, and press to stop the bleeding.

3 ◁ Apply a sterile dressing to the wound, but not so tightly as to impede circulation. Keep the arm elevated as it is being bandaged.

4 ◁ Beyond the bandage, check the circulation by pressing a nail bed until it is pale. On release, the color should return.

92 SHOCK

Shock is a dangerous reduction of blood flow around the body that may result in insufficient oxygen and nutrients reaching the tissues. Without swift treatment, the vital organs can fail, resulting in death.

HIDDEN DANGER
Internal bleeding may cause shock. If you suspect shock is due to this, monitor the victim continually.

CONSCIOUS VICTIM
Raise the feet higher than the head to help him stay conscious. Resuscitate (Tip 101) if breathing and heart stop.

Take pulse below radial artery

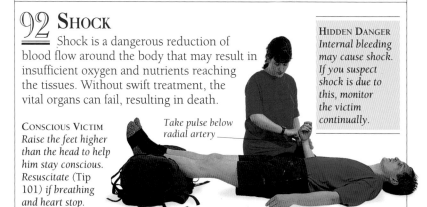

93 BURNS & SCALDS

Accidents with stoves, fires, and boiling water are the common causes of burns and scalds. Prompt action will prevent further tissue damage, so stop the burning, relieve the pain and swelling, and reduce the risk of infection at once. Do not remove anything stuck to the burn.

1 Flood the burn with cold water for at least 10 minutes to stop the burning and the pain.

2 To protect the area from infection, a clean plastic bag can be placed around the injury.

3 As soon as possible, replace the bag with a pad of gauze over the burn; secure with a bandage.

94 PROBLEMS CAUSED BY HEAT

In extreme heat, the thermostat in the brain can fail, resulting in a blood temperature above 104°F (40°C) – a condition known as heatstroke. Heat exhaustion is caused by a loss of salt and water from the body due to excessive sweating in a hot, humid environment.

Fan victim to keep him cool

Soak clothes in water to help reduce body heat

▽ HEAT EXHAUSTION
Give a salt solution: one teaspoon of salt per 2 pints (1 liter) of water. Place in recovery position if victim becomes unconscious.

Raise legs to improve circulation to vital organs

△ HEATSTROKE
Reducing the temperature of the victim is your priority in a case of heatstroke. If he loses consciousness, attempt resuscitation.

95 SUNBURN

Sunburn results from overexposure of the skin to direct sunlight. You are more prone to it when you spend all day walking outdoors. Sunburn causes redness, itching, tenderness, and blistering, and is very uncomfortable. The reflection of sunlight by water or snow increases the risk.

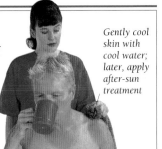

Gently cool skin with cool water; later, apply after-sun treatment

96 CRAMP

Cramp is a sudden, involuntary, and painful muscle spasm. It can be caused by heavy exercise, or by the loss of salt through excessive sweating, such as in heat exhaustion (*Tip 94*). To relieve cramp in the back of the thigh, straighten the victim's knee by raising the leg. For cramp in the front of the thigh, bend the knee. In each case, massage the muscle with your fingers.

Stretching toes upwards helps relieve cramp in calf

RAISE THE LEG
To relieve cramp in the victim's leg, raise it up toward you and bend the appropriate part of the leg.

97 VOMITING & DIARRHEA

Vomiting and diarrhea can cause severe dehydration. Make sure you maintain your fluid level by sipping often from a rehydration solution. This should consist of one teaspoon of salt and one table-spoon of sugar mixed with 2 pints (1 liter) of sterile or clean water.

98 COMBATING COLD

In cold conditions, always wear a hat to prevent rapid heat loss from the head and neck. When resting in a cold wind, immediately put on warm windproof clothing. Sit on your backpack to prevent heat loss to the ground, and hunch yourself up, hands in pockets, to conserve all your body heat.

99 HYPOTHERMIA

Hypothermia is a fall in body temperature to below 95°F (35°C). The treatment is to restore normal body temperature, 98.6°F (37°C), as soon as possible. Remove wet clothing and put the victim in dry clothes.

REASSURANCE
Help the victim to remove wet clothes and talk to him, giving reassurance.

Sleeping bag provides warmth

100 THE UNCONSCIOUS VICTIM

If the victim has lost consciousness, you need to assess whether his heart and lungs are functioning. You should follow the three steps of ABC: check Airway, Breathing, and Circulation. If you suspect a back or neck injury, make sure you first immobilize the head.

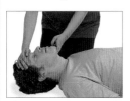

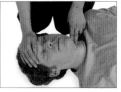

1 Open the victim's mouth and remove obstructions. Open the *Airway*, using the head-tilt/chin-lift technique, so one hand is on the forehead and the other is tilting the head back.

2 To detect *Breathing*, feel for exhaled breath against your cheek for 5 seconds. At the same time, watch for movements of the chest to indicate that the lungs are receiving air.

3 Check *Circulation* by feeling for a pulse for 5 seconds. If pulse and breathing are found, put in recovery position. If breathing is absent, begin RB; if both are absent, begin CPR (*Tip 101*).

Bent knee prevents victim from rolling

◁ THE RECOVERY POSITION
The arms and front leg are bent, the back leg straight. The head should be tilted back and the jaw forward, to open the airway.

101 RESUSCITATION TECHNIQUES

If the victim has stopped breathing but you can still detect a pulse, carry out rescue breathing by blowing air into the victim's lungs. If there is neither breathing nor a pulse, give cardiopulmonary resuscitation by regular chest compressions, to maintain the circulation of the blood, as well as rescue breathing.

RESCUE BREATHING (RB)

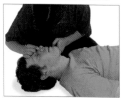

1 Lay the victim on his back and clear any obstructions from his mouth. With one hand on his forehead pinching his nose, and the other under his chin, tilt the head back.

2 Keeping his nose pinched with your index finger and thumb, seal your mouth over his and blow steadily into his lungs for 2 seconds. Remove your mouth and let his chest fully deflate.

3 Repeat Step 2, then give 10 breaths per minute. Continue this technique until help arrives, or until he is breathing by himself. Check for a pulse. If the pulse stops, begin CPR.

CARDIOPULMONARY RESUSCITATION (CPR)

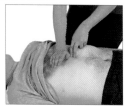

1 Lay the victim on a firm surface. Find one of his lowest ribs with your index and middle fingers, then follow it up until your middle finger lies where the rib meets the breastbone.

2 Your index finger now lies on the breastbone. Slide the heel of your other hand down the breastbone until it touches your index finger. This is where you apply the pressure.

3 Place one hand over the other, lacing the fingers. With straight arms, press down firmly, then release without removing your hands. Give 15 compressions, then 2 breaths of RB.

INDEX

ACKNOWLEDGMENTS

Dorling Kindersley would like to thank Hilary Bird
for compiling the index, Alison Copland for proofreading,
Melissa Albany for picture research, Mark Bracey and
Robert Campbell for DTP assistance, and Lang & Hunter,
Richmond and Kingston branches, for the loan of equipment.

Photography
KEY: t *top*; b *bottom*; c *center*; a *above*; l *left*; r *right*
Main photography by Andy Crawford, Steve Gorton, and
Tim Ridley. Additional photographs by Max Alexander, Jane Burton,
Joe Cornish, Tim Daley, Neil Fletcher, Paul Harris, Dave King,
Roger Moss, Susanna Price, Alan Williams, Peter Wilson.

The publisher would like to thank the following for their kind
permission to reproduce their photographs:
Bruce Coleman: Jeff Foot 60ca; Hans Reinhard bl; Imagebank:
Stockphotos Inc./Simon Wilkinson 2; Mountain Camera:
John Cleare 11 cra, 11br, 18cl, 34tr, 46tr, 48tr, 49tr; NHPA:
NH Callow 60crb; Stockshot: Jeff Stock 46cr, 46 clb;
Telegraph Colour Library: S. Markewitz 46br;
Tony Stone Images: Paul Chesley 62 tr; Zefa 6bl, 8bl.

Illustrations & Maps
All illustrations by Coral Mula, except Norman Lacey 44.
Maps by James Anderson, James Mills-Hicks, and John Plumer
of Dorling Kindersley Cartography.